Ivan P. Barsukov

The life and work of Innocent, the archbishop of Kamchatka

Ivan P. Barsukov

The life and work of Innocent, the archbishop of Kamchatka

ISBN/EAN: 9783744640466

Printed in Europe, USA, Canada, Australia, Japan

Cover: Foto ©Andreas Hilbeck / pixelio.de

More available books at **www.hansebooks.com**

Translated from the Russian and printed
for distribution among the people
by request of
THE MOST REVEREND BISHOP NICHOLAS

Cubery & Co., Printers, 587 Mission St., S. F.

INNOCENTIUS, Archbishop of Kamchatka, the Kuriles and the Aleutian Islands, the ever memorable preacher of Christianity in the extreme East, was elevated to the vacant See of Moscow in 1867, on the demise of the celebrated Metropolitan Philaret. From the distant shores of the Amoor he went direct to the first capital city of Moscow—the heart of Russia.

The town of Anginskoe in the Government of Irkoutsk was the home of Innocentius. The register of the church in Anginskoe shows that "on the 26th of August (old style), 1797, the wife of the sacristan of the church of St. Elias the Prophet, Eusebius Popov, bore him a son who was named John." At five years of age John Popov commenced to study his alphabet, being instructed by his father, who was at the time already afflicted with the disease which brought on his death two years later, leaving a widow and four orphans in extreme poverty. Fortunately the uncle of the orphans, a deacon of the same church, Demetrius Popov, in order to help the orphaned family somewhat, took the little boy John into his own home and continued teaching him. The little one learned so rapidly that in his eighth year he read the epistles in church and by his clear reading afforded much consolation to the parishioners. The mother of the boy, observing her son's success, desired to obtain his father's vacancy for him, in order to support the family; but this did not come to pass. At nine years of age John Popov was brought to

Irkoutsk, where he was received as a scholar at the theological seminary.

At the seminary John surpassed all his schoolmates in learning. Tall of stature, with a good figure, and healthy, he was readily distinguished in their midst. At the time when John Popov entered the seminary, his uncle, with whom he previously lived, became a widower, and having taken the monastic vows with the name of David, he was transferred to Irkoutsk, making his home at the episcopal house, having also been ordained to the priesthood; and here, as before, he continued to care for his nephew, who often visited him. Father David was fond of mechanical labor; his nephew, coming to him, often found him at work on some machinery, and looking on assisted him, thus becoming very fond of the mechanical art himself.

At the seminary, during the time free of lessons, John always found occupation for himself; he would go somewhere apart from his schoolmates and read to himself, or else engage in building something. It was in this way he made in one of the rooms of the seminary a water-clock. The frame and wheels were made with a common knife and awl, the face was made of writing paper, the pointers of bits of wood. The water was poured into a pot of birch bark, and the dripping of it on a piece of tin beneath the pot sounded like the ticking of an ordinary clock; a bell sounded the hours. John's fellow - pupils were very much amused by this.

In 1814 a new rector of the seminary, guided by certain motives, thought it proper to change the surnames of the pupils. In giving names, the authorities generally considered some characteristic of the pupil, which assisted in making up the name; for instance, one who was good-looking consequently received the name Blagovidov (i. e. Good-looks); a pupil of quiet disposition was named Tihomirov (tihi is quiet, and mir is the world; the final *ov* or *off* denotes the possessive case and generally can be translated as *son*, for instance Johnson). Veniaminov was the name given to John Popov. He was named thus in honor of Benjamin, the Bishop of Irkoutsk, who was much loved by all, and who had died that same year. In 1817 John Veniaminov married, after which he was ordained a deacon for the Church of the Annunciation in Irkoutsk.

Graduating from the seminary John Veniaminov was appointed teacher of a parish school, and after a year ordained a priest for the same Church of the Annunciation. In the course of his service (which was short, a little over two years) he won the esteem and love of his people as a good shepherd who cares for his flock. The inhabitants of Irkoutsk long remembered the even and grand church services of Father John, likewise his kindly nature and pastoral cares. On Sundays, before the liturgy, he would gather the children in the church and instruct them in Christian lessons.. Only two years passed thus, in which he enjoyed his quiet home life; soon he must change it for a life full of privations, trouble, heavy labor and glorious undertakings.

In 1823 the Most Holy Synod requested the Bishop of Irkoutsk to send a priest to the Island Ounalashka, for the purpose of enlightening the natives with the faith of Christ. Ounalashka and the neighboring islands lie out a long distance from Siberia, between Kamchatka and America. The Prelate informed the clergy of Irkoutsk, but no one was found to accept the Holy Synod's offer. No one desired to go to a strange and distant land. The Bishop was put in an awkward position; the order of the Synod must be carried out, yet no volunteers were found, and he could not send any one against his will. Then it was that the priest of the Annunciation (parish), Father John Veniaminov came to His Right Reverence and informed him of his willingness to go to Ounalashka. The Bishop was not a little surprised at this; he was sorry to give up an exemplary clergyman.

It must be remembered that at the time this announcement was sent to the clergy by the Bishop, Father Veniaminov, as well as all the clergy, did not so much as think of accepting it. It happened that Father John about this same time became acquainted with a certain John Kriukov, who had come to Irkoutsk from Ounalashka. This newcomer, Kriukov, from the coast of America, had much to tell him of Ounalashka and of life out there and he went so far as to persuade him to accept the Bishop's offer. But no persuasion affected him. How it was that Father John became taken with the desire to go to such a distant land, many years after he tells of it himself in these words: ⌐ "When that pioneer, John Kriukov, had already bidden me good-bye, and on his farewell-taking still continued to persuade me to go to Ounalashka—and on the same day, taking leave of the Bishop (in whose presence I happened to be then) he commenced telling of the devotion of the Aleuts to prayer and to listening to the Word of God (may the name of the Lord be blessed); I suddenly, it can be said, and completely became inflamed with the desire to go to such a people. I now vividly call to memory, how I suffered with impatience, waiting for the moment when I could inform His Right Reverence of my intention, and he seemed to be surprised, saying only: we shall see." ⌐

After a long hesitation the Bishop at last consented. The family of Father John did not so much as suspect the rapid change in his determination. On coming home Father John said nothing of his intentions to his family. But of course, such a sudden turn in his fate could not but reflect itself on him, so that it became apparent to those around him. During one of the family conversations, his little son, somewhat over a year old, came up to him. Father John took him up in his arms. "My child," said he, "where will your feet soon be a-walking." Now only was it that his family surmised at what had happened; they fell upon him with tears and wailings, begging him to alter his decision. But he remained steadfast. They commenced to prepare for the long, strange journey.

On the 7th of May, 1823, Father John left Irkoutsk with his family, which then consisted of his old mother, his wife, a son a year old, and a brother.

First of all he went to his home, in rural Anginskoe, and from there, having offered a prayer-service, took a barge going down the river Lena to Yakoutsk.

The Lena is the largest river in Siberia and flows into the Arctic Ocean.

From Yakoutsk Father John had to ride to Ohotsk, a city in Eastern Siberia, on the shore of the Sea of Ohotsk. The distance between Yakoutsk and Ohotsk is one thousand versts, or about 700 miles, and he made all that way with his family, on horseback. The road was a difficult one; now he would ride by narrow trails through dense forests, then he would make his way over such marshy land, that a horse would sink into it to its belly, and at other times he must climb along a slope, or a steep, rocky mountain and move along its slippery back covered with snow. Yet with God's help Father John patiently overcame all these hardships. At last the travelers heard the dull roar of sea waves breaking against the high cliffs on the coast. The masts of vessels on the Ohotsk River gradually appeared to them, and then the city of Ohotsk itself. From Ohotsk to the Island of Ounalashka Father John made the voyage in a sailing vessel. On the 29th of July, 1824, he safely arrived at the place of his appointment.

II.

Ounalashka is one of the Aleutian Islands. These Islands lie in the Pacific Ocean between Kamchatka and Alaska. Ounalashka is about the largest island in the Aleutian group. It is 150 versts in length and more than fifty in width.

The climate on this Island, as well as on the others, is damp and changeable. Cloudy weather with fogs and winds is the condition for the most part of the year, while clear and bright days are very rare, not more than fifty of them throughout the year. The summer here is not too warm, but in winter the frosts are sometimes so severe as to frost-bite a flying bird.

Besides the Aleutian Islands there were others also which belonged to the parish of Father John; among them were the Fox, the Pribilov and other Islands.

The native inhabitants of all these islands are employed in hunting fur-animals and fishing. They live in villages of earthen huts,* which appear more like bear haunts than human habitations. In the day time the interior of the hut obtains its light from a window in the roof, through which also the smoke escapes, but at night a fire burns in the center of the hut, which heats it also.

The wealthy Aleuts have the walls of their huts covered with furs and skins; no furniture or seats provided, they sit upon the floor. Their utensils they seldom wash, although they cook and wash their clothes in the same. The Aleuts are an unclean people.

In appearance the Aleuts are homely and have poor features; they are of middle stature, but on first sight they appear to be very short, because of the fact that the

---

*This was before the Russians had fully succeeded in obtaining the necessary materials for building, which are not provided by nature in the Alaskan Islands.

knees of all of them are bent in consequence of their continual posture on the floor, or sitting in a baidarka (canoe). They walk with the points of their feet turning in, while their heels spread outwards. It is impossible for a Russian to walk in the path made by an Aleut. These people are good and soft-hearted. In time of want, and during the winters a famine is nothing new with them; should any one of them be able to obtain some food, he will be sure to divide it among them all. They show much attention and love for their parents and elders. They are very hardy and patient. It seems impossible to think of any hardship that an Aleut could not bear, or of any sorrow that would make him melancholy. In time of want it is nothing extraordinary for him to live on water alone for three and four days. In sickness, when suffering excruciating pain, you will not hear him utter a cry nor a sigh.

Up to the time of the arrival of Father John the Aleuts were in a wild condition, and in religious belief they were half idol worshippers. Father John had found but one chapel in Ounalashka on his arrival there, and that was an old wooden one. His first work was to build a new church. Being himself a good carpenter and builder, he began teaching the natives these handicrafts, and as soon as they were sufficiently proficient, he commenced building the church. At that he took a lively personal interest in the work, and made with his own hands the holy table and ikonostasis,* which he gilded. The church was dedicated in honor of the Ascension of the Lord. At the same time Father John Veniaminov undertook a great and difficult task— the study of the native languages. He desired to translate for the aborigines the Gospel and the liturgy, and—

*A screen with the images of our Lord, the Apostles, etc., separating the altar from the body of the temple.

as we shall see hereafter—he accomplished the undertaking. We call this work remarkable, for the reason that he had to undergo the labor of inventing the very alphabet itself, which these languages never had. Studying the Aleutian language, Father John endeavored to acquaint himself with their traditions and customs, in order to be better understood when preaching to them the Word of God. He could often be seen conversing with those who were converted before he came to the island, and also with the pagan natives, about the true religion.

He preached sermons to them adapted to their understanding; he explained the meaning of the different feasts, confession and holy communion, also repeating how necessary it is to often attend church services.

Eye-witnesses recall to memory the sermon that Father John preached on the Sunday of Cheese-Fare, on February 9th, 1828, which also happened to be the day of St. Innocentius, the Wonder-worker of Irkoutsk. The great multitude of hearers were impressed and moved to tears by the sincere words and humility of this priest. First he explained the meaning of fast and showed the difference between the primitive Christians and those of today. "The Christians of old" said Father John Veniaminov, "with great joy looked forward and awaited the coming of holy Lent, as they knew the power and benefit of Lent, and they understood wherefore it was instituted—and they knew not only with their mind, or by hearing, but by the very sense of feeling (experience). But many of the christians of today, with sorrow see the approach of the time of fast, because they do not see, and do not know, or do not care to know and see the power and benefit of Lent." Then the preacher put the question: "Why was it that Lent was instituted, and how can we fulfill the duties which it exacts of us?" Explaining this question, he then continued:

"Our Orthodox Church (Græco-Russian) follows the custom of asking forgiveness on this day for the offenses done one to another, as the time of Great Lent is come, during which we must beg forgiveness of the Heavenly Father. In fulfilling this holy practice, I, your unworthy pastor, ask of you, my brethren, the forgiveness of all with which I have sinned before you, if by word, or in deed, or in my life; may God by His grace forgive and have mercy upon us all. I advise you also, brethren, to fulfill this duty now, and to always keep the practice hereafter. We should forgive and ask forgiveness sincerely and correctly, and not in outward appearance, falsely. Moreover, the holy Church—our Mother, advises and requests us—and the duty of christianity demands of us—to keep this holy Lent, to cleanse our conscience from (the stain of) evil works by true repentance. And in this way, with a pure soul and heart, we shall go forward to meet the great day of the glorious Resurrection."

It was not only with the sermons which he preached near his home, that Father John served his charge. His parish was widely scattered, over several thousand versts; he had to sail from island to island, from one village to another. To these voyages Father Veniaminov gave a good part of the year. His patience and intrepidity while traveling are truly worthy of admiraation. He suffered privations and risked danger sailing from island to island, over the ocean waves in a little boat (baidarka—an Aleutine canoe made of skin), so narrow, that he must outstretch his limbs and keep them so, as if they were bound together in swaddling clothes. Sometimes Father John was obliged to suffer hunger and cold, and again, being caught in a sweeping rain, wet to the bone, he would have to lodge in a dirty and cold earthen hut. Arriving at a village of Aleuts, if it was convenient Father John performed the Church services, or simply gathered together the inhabitants and taught them the Word of God and advised them to receive baptism. But he never administered to them the Sacrament of Baptism, until they had asked for it themselves.

Having acquired the Aleutian language Father John invented an alphabet for it and little by little commenced to translate for his people the sacred books. This way he translated into the Aleutian language the catechism and the Gospel of St. Matthew. In order to teach the Aleuts how to read and write, he opened a school on the Island of Ounalashka for boys and taught them himself.

Father Veniaminov loved the Aleuts for their simpleheartedness and diligence in hearing the Word of God; and the Aleuts also loved their pastor, and were sincerely devoted to him for his good nature and for the kindness he showed them. " Of all the good qualities of the Aleuts," Father John would say, " nothing gave me more pleasure and satisfied my heart than the diligence they had for listening, or more properly the thirst they had for hearing the Word of God, for a most untiring preacher could become weary sooner than their diligence become lessened. Let us explain this by an example. On my arrival in a village, one and all, leaving their work and occupations at my first call, at once gathered to hear me preach, and listening with wonderful attention, not allowing themselves to become restless or even to turn their eyes from me. The most tender mothers seemed at such moments to grow hardened at the cry of their children, of whom only those were brought along that were able to understand. I acknowledge openly that during such conversations (or preaching), I experienced in fact the consolations of the christian faith, those sweet and unspeakable touches of grace, and therefore I owe the Aleuts more thanks than they owe me for my work, and I will never forget them."

On the Island of Ounalashka Father John at first
lived with his family in an earthen hut, then in a small
wooden house, which he built with his own hands. The
furniture, the clock on the wall, were his own make; in
a word, when it was necessary, he became carpenter,
mechanic, watch-maker, and sometimes a maker of fishing nets. The evenings Father Veniaminov sometimes
would spend in mechanical work, or in teaching his own
children, to whom he was most kind. Not only his own
children, but other children as well, he loved, and he
could often be seen surrounded by them, explaining to
them some lessons from Sacred History or the Gospel
in his simple way, and with language easily understood,
or at other times playing at ball with them. He would
ramble with the children in the hills, and as a lover and
observer of nature, he would share with them his
knowledge. Besides such occupations Father John
with his children would make the candles for their
church.

In such constant labor and cares Father John Veniaminov passed ten years on the Island of Ounalashka.
During that time he converted to christianity all the
inhabitants of the island. The toil and noble undertakings of this good priest could not remain unnoticed
on the part of the authorities, and he was rewarded
with a pectoral cross. Then he was transferred to the
Port of New Archangel, or Sitkha (on Baranov Island),
that he might convert another people—the Kolosha-s.

III.

Sitkha or New Archangel is a good distance from the
Aleutian Islands, and lies almost within touch of the
mainland of America.

The climate here is noted for being damp, and during most part of the year the weather is gloomy and foggy. The soil on this island (now, known as Baranov—the name of one of the Governors) is marshland and partly stone, covered with a thin layer of putrefied matter. Novoarhangelsk is situated on the western coast of the island, and at that time it was the central headquarters for the government of the Russian Colonies in America. Novoarhangelsk (New Archangel) or Sitkha is surrounded by mountains, which are covered with forests of tall trees of the fir species. It should be mentioned that the woods of this Sitkha (the Indian name) or Bar - anov Island are of a wonderful growth, some of the trunks of spruce measuring 150 feet in length.

The inhabitants of this Island—the Kolosha (or Thlinket tribe of Alaskan Indians), among whom the Reverend Father Veniaminov had now to labor, differed from the Aleuts in appearance as well as in character. In appearance they are handsome: they have large black eyes, correct face, black hair, and are of medium stature. The Kolosha has a proud and selfish nature. On visiting the Russians they would don their best apparel and maintain a haughty bearing. They are very revengeful; if a Kolosha for some reason could not avenge himself during his life for some offense, he would transmit his revenge to his generation. The Kolosha possess a lively mind and they are sagacious.

They were less acquainted with the christian religion than the Aleuts. Towards the Russians, especially before this time, they were hostile, and such a bearing greatly impeded the spread of Christianity among them.

After his arrival in Sitkha, Father John commenced work in the same way he had done on the Island of Ounalashka, i. e. he began by learning the language and customs of the Koloshas, and then proceeded to preach the Word of God to them. At the same time, as was

his wont, he gave freely of his labor, his strength, his
health. As in Ounalashka, now also he often preached
to his congregation in the church, and when possible
visited them in their homes, and there in the family—
as a father among his children—he told them of the
Orthodox religion. The Kolosha learned to love their
teacher, and commenced to receive him with a welcome,
willingly and attentively listening to his lessons.

Living among the Koloshas, Father John wrote sermons for them in their native tongue and translated the
sacred books, which helped much in spreading Orthodoxy among them. The labor of the Reverend John
Veniaminov was not lost; the result was that the number of christians in that country increased very rapidly.

For five years Father John worked on Baranov
Island (Sitkha). His fifteen years of active missionary
life (first in Ounalashka, then in Sitkha) was distinguished with the zeal that made famous the first teach-
ers of the Gospel. He always went about his work
with great care, and thereby drew to himself the rough
hearts of the savages; he would convince, but not urge,
then patiently wait for their own petition, asking for
baptism. For the children Father John opened schools,
and taught them from books he had himself compiled.
Finally, besides enlightening the natives with the
knowledge of the Gospel, he taught them the different
trades of smith-craft and carpentry, and also introduced
inoculation (to prevent epidemics among them). In
this way he won the · hearty sympathy; the Indians
loved him. And he really was their benefactor and
teacher.

Many years of experience in missionary work con-
vinced our preacher that it was difficult to keep the
spirit of Christianity animated in a country, already
containing a large number of the baptized, and in which
the native villages are so scattered. For this, continual

exhortation was necessary, and yet it was impossible through the lack of priests and insufficiency of means. In order to remove these hindrances, and this could be done by the authority of the Church Government, it was necessary to take steps and intercede. And so Father John decided to go to St. Petersburg for this purpose. Besides this he must apply personally for permission to print his Aleutian translations of the sacred books. Having thus decided, Father John took a leave of absence, and—sending his wife and children to their home in Irkoutsk—on the 8th of November, 1838, he left Sitkha, taking sail in a globe circumnavigating vessel. His voyage continued for eight months; on the 25th of June, 1839, Father John arrived in St. Petersburg and presented his petition for the decision of the Most Holy Synod. Learning that it would take some months before the question of his petition would be taken up, he occupied himself in collecting offerings for the purpose of propagating and confirming the Christian religion in the Aleutian Islands, and for this he went also to Moscow.

In Moscow he presented himself to the Most Reverend Philaret, the Metropolitan—Archbishop. At first sight the Prelate took a liking for the hardworking, industrious missionary. "There is something apostle-like in this man"—he would say when speaking of Father John. More than once, when time permitted, they conversed together alone and the Prelate would listen with interest to the wonderful stories Father John told of his life in the Aleutian Islands. In the fall our traveler returned to St. Petersburg and he was promoted to the office of Archpriest for his long apostolic labors.

But at this time he received the sad news, informing him of the death of his wife. This sorrow weighed heavily upon him. The Metropolitan Philaret, consoling him, advised him to take vows and enter the monastic state.. This proposal compelled the Father Archpriest to stop and deeply consider. He could not make up his mind, because his six children—two sons and four daughters—seemed to hold him in check; he had no one to entrust them to and no where to settle them. Not consenting to the proposition of Metropolitan Philaret he went to Kiev in order to pray there and pay his reverence to those miraculous shrines. On his return from Kiev he was summoned before the Most Holy Synod, and when here advised to take the vows of a monk, he consented, giving himself up to the will of God. His children, at Philaret's request, were settled in the best possible manner.

On the 29th of November, 1840, the Archpriest John Veniaminov, entering the monastic order, was tonsured and given the name of Innocent; at the same time he was ordered as an Archimandrite (an abbot with the privilege of wearing a miter). In the meantime the Holy Synod had concluded to organize a new diocese in Alaska. The question arose as to who should be the bishop of the new diocese. The names of three selected candidates were presented to the Emperor Nicholas Pavlovich, one of which was that of the Archimandrite Innocentius. The Sovereign desired to see him. Having received the newly appointed Archimandrite kindly, the Emperor, bidding him adieu, said to him: "Tell the Metropolitan it is my desire that you be appointed bishop for the new diocese."

The consecration of the Right Reverend Innocent in the episcopal order took place on the 15th of December, 1840, in St. Petersburg, in the grand church of our Lady of Kazan. "I firmly hope and believe," said Innocentius at the time of his installation as a newly-elect Bishop, "that the Lord, who has guided me so long and now is giving me this new lot of service, will by His grace give me also new and greater strength for the accomplishment of the same. I pray you, the Godly selected fathers and guardians of the Church upon earth, to give me a place in your prayers, praying to the Lord in my behalf, that His grace and mercy be with me evermore." The 10th of January, 1841, was the day on which Bishop Innocent left St. Petersburg to go to his church in Alaska.

On his way back he visited Irkoutsk. One can imagine with what feeling the Right Reverend Innocent entered his native city, and with what joy and veneration the population of Irkoutsk must have received one of their former pastors—John Veniaminov, who now was an Archpastor. The people met him in crowds on entering the city; the bells on every church chimed. The Bishop visited the Church of the Annunciation, where he formerly served as a priest, and offered the Liturgy and a thanksgiving service. Having left Irkoutsk he stopped on his way in his native Anginskoe, went into the cottage in which he was born and where his childhood was spent, visited his old acquaintances, and—having offered a service of supplications—commenced his long journey, cheered with the well wishes of his countrymen. At last, on the 27th of September, 1841, after a long and tiresome voyage, Innocentius safely reached Sitkha, or the port of New Archangel.

IV.

Now after taking upon himself a new vocation, Bishop Innocent's work of spreading Christianity and enlightenment had greatly increased. He commenced by opening new parishes, the necessity of which by this time was strongly felt. Ordaining priests for the new parishes, the Right Rev. Innocent gave them the most minute instructions how to act, and requested them to convince by the power of the Word, but not with force or bribes.

Only seven months after his arrival in Novoarhangelsk (Baranov Island), Bishop Innocent again set sail for the purpose of voyaging through the diocese and inspecting it. He left the town of Sitkha on the 4th of May, 1842.

On every island, in each village, wherever the Bishop came, he was received with the greatest triumph and joy by the inhabitants; and in no place did he leave them without his episcopal instruction. On the 18th of August, 1842, he landed in the Port of Petropavlovsk, Kamchatka.

Petropavlovsk is a small town surrounded by mountains and situated on their slope by the water—on the Bay of Avachin. The houses here are built in the same fashion that we find them in all eastern Siberia. The haven, broad and convenient for vessels, is known to navigators as one of the largest in the world. In Petropavlovsk Bishop Innocent remained for four months, awaiting the wintry season for journeying. Finally on the 29th of November the great journey of Innocentius through Kamchatka commenced. The Archpriest Gromov, who was one of the travelers, going over the snow in dog sleighs, describes the journey in these words: "There are three kinds of conveyances which are used in journeys over the snow, and which are drawn by dogs. The first is the *sanka*—this is nothing else than a saddle made of twigs and rods fixed on thin slides. The second is a *narta*—very much like a child's sled, only much larger, and then the *povozochka*, also a narta with the addition of a box it has fixed upon it which is made of deer skin or canvas. Some of the better povozochki contain a window in the covering made of glass or mica, so that during long voyages one may read and not feel so much the irksomeness. On the sanka only one person can sit, and it is used for light drives. The narta is used for transferring heavy weights, and the povozochka for the carrying of important personages and the higher officials. In this last conveyance only one person can sit, and at that in such a position that he cannot move or turn. On the front the *Kayour* (driver) sits supplied with a pole, whicn serves in his hands as a balance over uneven roads, and as a brake on going down hill. For the sanka five dogs are sufficient, but for the narta and povozochka from fourteen to twenty dogs must be harnessed. They are tied in pairs to a long strap which is attached to the sleigh, and this sort of a coach flits along like an arrow over the snow-drifts. The dogs are controlled by the voice of the kayour, gkah, gkah (to the right), gkuh, gkuh (to the left), hna (stop) but for trained dogs it is sufficient, without using the voice, to strike with the pole on one or the other side of the sleigh and they will turn to the right or left accordingly."

By means of these dog-sleds the Right Reverend Innocent had traveled over 5000 versts. " One cannot imagine—say those who traveled in Kamchatka—all the hardships of the traveler who is drawn only by dogs for several hundred miles over a snowy plain, when the thermometer falls to twenty below zero in a Siberian frost. For the safety of travelers in a snowstorm, which sometimes lasts for several days in succession, log huts at every forty or fifty versts are built, and in these they pass the night. In these huts, which are not made well, a stone fireplace can be found. But it often happens that travelers cannot reach such a shelter before night; they then dig into the snow till they reach the ground, which makes a kind of cave, at the entrance of which they light a fire, and in this way, in a most severe frost, they are compelled to pass the night."

On the 3rd of April, 1843, Bishop Innocent arrived in Ohotsk, where he remained for about four months; at that time he was spreading the Faith among the Koriak, Chukcha and the Tunguz.

At last the first journey of Bishop Innocent was finished, and he safely arrived in Novoarhangelsk, where he occupied himself in bringing to order his young diocese But this was not his last tour of inspection; he had made three such voyages and journeys, during which he carefully examined the newly organized parishes, consecrated churches, personally preached the word of God to the natives and—where it was possible —opened schools for the children. For his good work in 1850 Innocentius was raised to the dignity of an Archbishop.

The success in spreading Christianity on the distant borders of Asia and America by the Most Reverend Innocent was the reason why the higher government of the church added to his diocese the country of the Yakout, with the inhabitants of which he earlier became acquainted. On this account Archbishop Innocent had to change the place of his residence from Novoarhangelsk, or Sitkha, to the city of Yokoutsk in Siberia.

Living in Yakoutsk the Prelate took much pains in supervising the translation of the sacred books into the Yakout language. Great was the day for the Yakout people, when at last the first Liturgy was offered in their native language.

The Archbishop himself officiated at the praise service and read the Gospel. This event had so touched the hearts of the Yakouts that their native representatives came to the Prelate Innocent with their petition, asking that this day forever be kept as a holiday, because it was the first on which they heard in the temple, the Divine teaching in their own tongue.

From Yakoutsk the Archbishop, not considering his old age, often undertook journeys over his great diocese which now had become much more widened, exposing himself to privations and dangers. During one of these journeys, when in the port of Ayan, he was nearly captured by the English, who suddenly took possession of that town, they being then at war with Russia.

At the end of June, 1857, the Most Reverend Innocent was summoned to St Petersburg for the purpose of taking part in the councils of the Most Holy Synod. During his sojourn in the Capital an Imperial High Degree had been issued, granting two Vicars (assistant Bishops to an Archbishop), one for Yakoutsk and the other for Sitkha. In this way the labors of the Venerable Archbishop were made lighter.

The Most Reverend Innocent left St. Petersburg in the beginning of 1858, but before going to Yakoutsk he traveled through the Amoor Country, which was then annexed to Russia. The great Amoor River flows for several thousand versts and separates the Chinese boundary line from the Russian. During this journey the Archbishop stopped in almost every town by the River and held services. But what was still more simple, he would sometimes on passing a village give orders to land, and then he would commence to teach the inhabitants who had run together on the beach. And nothing on these occasions was hid from the Prelate; he entered into all the cares and needs of his people, both the spiritual and the bodily.

In 1862 the Most Reverend Innocent took up his home in the town of Blagoveshchensk on the banks of the Amoor. Here also he continued untiringly to fulfill the duties of his office, endeavoring much to firmly plant Orthodoxy in the diocese. From this place he likewise often undertook journeys along the Amoor and into other districts, personally inspecting and instructing the newly converted. But old age and poor health already compelled him to think of rest. He asked to be relieved and to be given quarters for rest. But his pastoral cares were not to be ended this time, and the will of God prepared for him another duty.

In 1867 Philaret, the Metropolitan of Moscow, had passed into eternity, and for a long time it could not be decided as to who should be appointed successor to the great Prelate. At last the election was held; the Archbishop Innocent was appointed to succeed the deceased Metropolitan. The Most Reverend Innocent was shocked with greater surprise than any one else. Having read the dispatch, he changed in the face, and for some minutes fell into deep thought. He then secluded himself for that day, and during the night he prayed long and fervently upon his knees. He was taken with wonder over his own destiny; the son of a poor village sexton, who at one time was unable to become the sacristan in place of his father, comes to be one of the first hierarchs in the great Russian Church—a Metropolitan in Moscow!

In sincere humility, notwithstanding his poor health, Archbishop Innocent accepted his new appointment and began to prepare for the way.

It would be needless to say with what expressions of joy and veneration the inhabitants of the cities of Siberia had met and seen him off on the way through which he must pass. It was the first time in their life they had seen a Metropolitan, and the last, as the Prelates who are invested with such high dignity, do not visit these distant places. With especial triumph he was waited upon in his own native Irkoutsk, where, owing to washouts, he had to remain for a considerable time, during which he offered the Liturgy several times, together with other Bishops who were there. Finally at 9:30 o'clock, on the evening of the 25th of May, 1868, the ringing bells heard all over Moscow announced that the new Archpastor had arrived in the capital. On the next day the Most Reverend Innocentius, Metropolitan of Moscow and Kolomna, officially entered the great Church of the Assumption. On entering the Cathedral the Prelate delivered an address which was full of true humility.

"Who am I—he said—to dare to take the word and the power of my predecessors? A pupil of distant times, of a remote country, who passed more than half a life time on the frontiers; one who is only a common worker in Christ's vineyard, a teacher of children and of those who are new in the Faith."

With such humility did the Metropolitan Innocent enter into his new office. He was now more than seventy years of age, worn with sickness, nearly blind, yet he was full of strength and zeal for activity. Administering to the government of his new diocese, by his care he did much that was beneficial. He erected asylums for widows and orphans, organized different benevolent societies, sought to alleviate the condition of the poor clergy, took measures for the better education of the populace, and besides all this, sat in the Council of the Holy Synod, taking part in ministering the spiritual affairs of all Russia. On the 18th of May, 1871, exactly fifty years had passed from the day on which John Veniaminov was ordained a priest, and the whole body of the Clergy of the Diocese of Moscow tendered their heartfelt congratulations to the Metropolitan.

But in the midst of pastoral work and cares old age and bodily ailments already began to tell upon the Most Reverend Innocent Finally sickness entirely weakened him, when on the 30th of March, 1879, he called to his bedside the house-warden, the Hieromouach Arsenius, that he may read for him the office said at the departure of a soul, and at 2 o'clock, on the morning of the 31st of March, Innocentius had passed away.

"Tell them—he said, dying—that no eulogies be pronounced at my funeral; they only contain praise. Let them rather preach a sermon; it may be instructive; and here is the text for it: '*The ways of man are ordered by the Lord.*'"

At 11 o'clock the next day the great bell in the tower of Ivan the Great pealed forth the announcement to the citizens of Moscow, that the Prelate was dead. On the 5th of April the body of the reposed was buried in the ground by the side of the grave of the Metropolitan Philaret in the Troitse—Sergiev Monastery.

And long will Russia remember this great worker, who planted the Faith of Christ among so many Pagan tribes in the most distant and severe countries, truly with saintly patience, with meekness and remarkable humility. For an example of such humility, and such simple words, which are penetrated with pure, fervent faith, we have a small book written by Metropolitan Innocent, and it is: *Showing the Way to the Kingdom of Heaven*. It is pointed out in this splendid book, how we may fulfill the word of the Savior—take the cross and follow him—how we may receive the Holy Ghost, how we may destroy the wall of sins, which separates us from our Redeemer and the Kingdom of Heaven.

In the realms of God's eternal mansions,

Now thou restest, faithful planter of His missions.

No words of ours can justly honor thee in a praise of rhyme;

On high we look and behold thy halo, truly apostolic and sublime.

Corona of glory, Innocent, teacher of the Aleut, and the Indian's friend!

Ever blessed in the memory of the Kamchadal and the Yakout who are by thee gladdened.

Note also this gathering and the joy of all thy people on the hundreth anniversary of thy birth;

The Orthodox Church in wide America exults, because thy Alaskan Diocese was her birth.